Unto Us

A Christmas Pageant

Claracy L. M. Waldrop

BROADMAN PRESS
Nashville, Tennessee

To the Memory

Of My Beloved Husband

Earl Leo Waldrop

(1902-1956)

This Pageant Is Affectionately Dedicated

Nashville, Tennessee

4297-04
ISBN: 0-8054-9704-8

Printed in the United States of America
Library of Congress catalog card number 57—10299

FOREWORD

In its conception and writing this pageant lends itself to the simplest or most extravagant production—a completely bare stage with simple draperies, "a space stage technique" (flooding various areas with spotlights), or insert sets, or a combination of all three. A platform, approximately 6 by 12 feet, may be used, remaining in its upstage-center position throughout.

Seven spotlights are needed: two on the downstage-right area, two on the downstage-left area, one center stage, and two upstage-center. The upstage spots are used to indicate the presence of angels.

Two readers will be needed, the first a woman and the second a man.

CHARACTERS:

- TWO READERS
- ISAIAH
- MICAH
- MARY
- JOSEPH
- THREE SHEPHERDS
- THREE WISE MEN

UNTO US

The service opens with the singing of "O Come, All Ye Faithful" by the audience.

As the hymn is finished, house lights are turned off and side spots light up the two readers, one on either side. After the first tableau curtains are opened, the spots are taken off the readers and they use small lights which fit onto their lecterns.

Introduction

First Reader: How beautiful upon the mountains are the feet of him that bringeth good tidings, that publisheth peace.

Second Reader: That bringeth good tidings of good, that publisheth salvation; that saith unto Zion, Thy God reigneth!

First Reader: Thy watchman shall lift up the voice; with the voice together shall they sing: for they shall see eye to eye, when the Lord shall bring again Zion.

Second Reader: Break forth into joy, sing together, ye waste places of Jerusalem: for the Lord hath comforted his people, he hath redeemed Jerusalem. The Lord hath made bare his holy arm in the eyes of all the nations; and all the ends of the earth shall see the salvation of our God.

First Tableau

The Prophecy

(When the curtain opens and the narrator begins, a spotlight is focused on Isaiah, who is seated on a long, low bench in front of a backdrop on which are painted large stones. This setting represents a city gate. He may hold a scroll in his hand.

Micah stands on the opposite side of the stage from Isaiah.)

Curtain opens

(Spotlight on Isaiah)

FIRST READER: Hear the voice of the prophet Isaiah.

SECOND READER: For unto us a child is born, unto us a son is given: and the government shall be upon his shoulder: and his name shall be called Wonderful, Counsellor, The mighty God, The everlasting Father, The Prince of Peace.

(Spotlight on Micah)

FIRST READER: Hear the voice of the prophet Micah.

SECOND READER: But thou, Bethlehem Ephratah, though thou be little among the thousands of Judah, yet out of thee shall he come forth unto me that is to be ruler in Israel; whose goings forth have been from old, from everlasting . . .

And he shall stand and feed in the strength of the Lord, in the majesty of the name of the Lord his God; and they shall abide; for now shall he be great unto the ends of the earth.

Curtain

MUSIC: "It Came upon the Midnight Clear," stanza 1. Stanzas 2 and 4 may also be sung if time is needed to change the stage.

Second Tableau

THE ANNUNCIATION

(Use the downstage-left area with a three-fold flat suggesting a rustic cottage as the background, and a pin spot focused on Mary, who is seated on a small stool. A simpler setting—a three-fold screen with a very soft blue or rose cloth draped over it—can be used. Overhead spotlight indicates the presence of the angel.)

Curtain

First Reader: In the days when Rome was mistress of the world, there lived in the little village of Nazareth in Galilee a humble peasant girl whose name was Mary. She was betrothed to the young village carpenter, Joseph. Little is known about the girl Mary, but one day a marvelous thing happened. A divine messenger, in the form of the angel Gabriel, visited her and told her she had been chosen by God to become the mother of a child who should be the Saviour for whom the Jewish people had been looking for many centuries. When the angel visited her, he said: *(overhead spotlight on)*

Second Reader: "Fear not, Mary: for thou hast found favour with God. And, behold, thou shalt . . . bring forth a son, and shalt call his name Jesus. He shall be great, and shall be called the Son of the Highest: and the Lord God shall give unto him the throne of his father David: and he shall reign over the house of Jacob for ever; and of his kingdom there shall be no end."

First Reader: And Mary said, "Behold the handmaid of the Lord; be it unto me according to thy word." And the angel departed from her. And after the angel had departed, Mary mused and wondered how she, of all young women, was chosen for this experience. God could send Jesus in any wonderful way he chose, but he was to send him as a little child to live in a human home. And she was to be his mother. The knowledge of these things Mary hid in her heart, and faltered not in the divine ministry of mothering the only begotton Son of God. *(Mary sits meditating during music.)*

Music: "My Soul Doth Magnify the Lord," from Saint-Saens' *Christmas Oratorio* (trio); or Simpler's "Magnificat and Nunc Dimittis" (soprano solo); or an old French carol, "Now Sing We All Full Sweetly" (choir).

Curtain

Third Tableau

THE SHEPHERDS IN THE FIELD

(Use the center area for this tableau. At the back stand five small trees—real or cardboard—lighted from behind. A simple cluster of fir branches with shredded red and yellow crepe paper can be used to suggest a small fire. Use one spotlight on the group of three shepherds and one overhead spotlight to denote the presence of the angel.)

MUSIC: "While Shepherds Watched Their Flocks" (double quartet or choir).

Curtain opens

FIRST READER: Outside the little town of Bethlehem, which was only a few miles from the city of Jerusalem, there were some shepherds sitting on the hillside watching their flocks which were in the field. And an angel of the Lord came and stood by them, *(overhead spotlight on)* and the glory of the Lord shone round about them; and they were filled with terror. But the angel said to them:

SECOND READER: "Fear not: for, behold, I bring you good tidings of great joy, which shall be to all people. For unto you is born this day in the city of David a Saviour, which is Christ the Lord. And this shall be a sign unto you; Ye shall find the babe wrapped in swaddling clothes, lying in a manger."

FIRST READER: And suddenly there was with the angel a multitude of the heavenly host praising God, and saying, "Glory to God in the highest, and on earth peace, good will toward men."

MUSIC: "Glory to God" from *The Messiah,* or "Angels We Have Heard on High" ("Gloria in Excelsis Deo") (double quartet or choir).

SECOND READER: And it came to pass, as the angels were gone, the shepherds said one to another, "Let us now go even unto Bethlehem, and see this thing which the Lord hath made known unto us."

Curtain

MUSIC: "Hark! The Herald Angels Sing" (double quartet or choir).

Fourth Tableau

THE NATIVITY

(The tableau representing the manger scene might well be placed on a one-step platform, 6 feet by 12 feet. A three-fold screen covered with khaki blankets and old burlap bags serves as a background. Just in front of this screen is Mary, seated on a low stool. Joseph stands to the left of Mary. A very rustic crib of old wood, with straw and a rough coverlet in it, is in the center. Two cross spotlights focus on the crib. Straw is scattered on the floor of the platform.)

Curtain Opens

FIRST READER: Now this was the time of the year when everyone went to his own city to be enrolled for the tax, according to a decree from Caesar Augustus. And Joseph and Mary went up from Galilee, out of the city of Nazareth to Judea, unto the city of Bethlehem, to be taxed. And so it was, that, while they were there, she brought forth her firstborn son, and wrapped him in swaddling clothes, and laid him in a manger; because there was no room for them in the inn.

MUSIC: "No Candle Was There and No Fire" by Lehmann, or "Away in a Manger" (soprano soloist, accompanied by organ or harp if available).

Curtain

MUSIC: "O Little Town of Bethlehem" (double quartet or choir).

Fifth Tableau

THE VISIT OF THE SHEPHERDS

(The setting is the same as that for the fourth tableau, with the addition of spotlights on the shepherds, who stand one behind the other looking toward the manger.)

Curtain opens

SECOND READER: *(Begins as quickly as the curtain opens)* The shepherds hastened through the frosty, silent night until they came to Bethlehem, and there in the stable above which the star stood they found Mary and Joseph, and the babe lying in a manger. They stood in fear and reverence, gazing on this fulfilment of the angel's prophecy. After they had seen the child, they told everyone they saw what had been said to them about him, and all who listened were astonished at what the shepherds told them. Then they returned again to their flocks on the hillside, remembering the words which they had been told were spoken by the prophets many years before: For *unto us* a child is born, *unto us* a son is given, and his name shall be called Wonderful, Counsellor, The mighty God, The everlasting Father, The Prince of Peace.

Curtain

MUSIC: "Silent Night" (double quartet or choir).

Sixth Tableau

THE VISIT OF THE MAGI

(The three-fold flat used in the second tableau forms the background here. The manger is not used, since it is believed that some time elapsed before the Wise Men reached Bethlehem. A simple pallet of straw covered with a linen cloth should be used

for the Christ child's bed. A coverlet with a small pillow rolled inside it is laid on the pallet. Mary is seated on the stool with yarn or fabric in her hands as though she were weaving or sewing. The three Wise Men stand at right as the curtain opens.)

FIRST READER: Many prophecies had been made concerning the coming of the Messiah. Many wise men believed that Jesus would be born in Jerusalem; others, in Bethlehem. Of these wise men we know there were some who set out to follow the exceedingly bright new star which had appeared in the heavens. We do not know from what countries they may have come, but we do know that they came from the East. And when they arrived in Jerusalem, they asked:

SECOND READER: "Where is he that is born King of the Jews? for we have seen his star in the east, and are come to worship him."

FIRST READER: When Herod the king heard of the travelers, he was greatly troubled, and all the people in Jerusalem were, too. So Herod gathered together all the chief priests and scribes and anxiously asked them where the Christ should be born. And they said unto him, "In Bethlehem of Judea: for thus it is written by the prophet,

SECOND READER: And thou Bethlehem, in the land of Judah, art not the least among the princes of Judah: for out of thee shall come a Governor, that shall rule my people Israel."

FIRST READER: Then Herod called the Wise Men to him privately and asked them the exact time of the star's appearing. Then he sent them to Bethlehem and said, "Go and search diligently for the young child; and when ye have found him, bring me word again, that I may come and worship him also." And they, having heard the king, went their way.

Curtain opens

FIRST READER: And, lo, the star, which they saw in the east, went before them, till it came and stood over where the young child was. When they saw the star, they rejoiced with exceeding great joy. So they entered the house and saw the young child with Mary his mother, and fell down, and worshipped him. (*Three Wise Men kneel in worshipful attitude.*)

MUSIC: "We Three Kings of Orient Are," stanza 1 (male trio).

SECOND READER: Then opening their treasures, they offered unto him gifts. The first king brought a coffer of gold, the symbol of power, mayhap for a crown with which to honor this new uncrowned King.

MUSIC: "We Three Kings of Orient Are," stanza 2 (tenor solo).

(As this verse is being sung, the first king crosses at center, places the coffer of gold on the platform, and kneels in front and to the left of the platform.)

SECOND READER: The second king brought an urn of sweet, spicy incense, the symbol of prayer.

MUSIC: "We Three Kings of Orient Are," stanza 3 (bass solo).

(As this verse is being sung, the second king crosses center and places urn on platform, then kneels behind first king.)

SECOND READER: The third king brought a chalice of myrrh, a spice always used in the burial service and symbolic of death.

MUSIC: "We Three Kings of Orient Are," stanza 4 (baritone solo).

(As this verse is being sung, the third king places the chalice on platform but remains on stage right of Mary. Kneels.)

Curtains close slowly

MUSIC: "We Three Kings of Orient Are," stanza 5 (choir or double quartet).

Seventh Tableau

FINALE

(Setting is the same as for sixth tableau. Mary, holding the baby Jesus, sits on a low stool during the entire tableau.)

Curtain opens

FIRST READER: This, then, is the Saviour who came *unto us.*

SECOND READER: Let us worship him then with all our hearts, without doubting and fear, today, tomorrow, and forever.

ENTIRE AUDIENCE stands and sings "Joy to the World! The Lord Is Come." Curtains remain open until the last verse, and then

Curtains close very slowly

BENEDICTION

COSTUMES

See standard Bible pictures and follow the costuming as closely as possible, or consult such books as *Costuming a Play* by Elizabeth Grumball or *Biblical Costume* by Marian Logan Wright. The two prophets should be dressed in rich, colorful, tapestry robes, if possible.

Mary should be dressed in white, with a David-blue mantle draped over her head and hanging loosely around her shoulders. If a change is desired, a rose mantle can be worn in the sixth tableau.

The three shepherds should have coarse, thick, sunburned hair (wigs), or their heads can be covered with turban drapes. They should wear mantles of heavy, brown cloth or skins with broad belts around their waists.

Joseph should have black hair and beard. He wears a long russet (or any dark color) garment girdled at the waist. He wears sandals and turban-like headgear.

The three kings must be richly clad. It is easy to costume them in robes borrowed from local Shriners. The first king carries a coffer of gold. The second king carries an urn of incense. The third king carries a chalice of myrrh.